GUITAR

3-CHORD CHRISTMAS

ISBN 978-1-4950-2585-3

HAL•LEONARD®
CORPORATION
7777 W. BLUEMOUND RD. P.O. BOX 13819 MILWAUKEE, WI 53213

Visit Hal Leonard Online at
www.halleonard.com

Away in a Manger

Words by John T. McFarland (v.3)
Music by James R. Murray

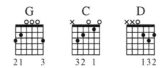

1. A - way in a man - ger, no crib for a bed, the
(2., 3.) *See additional lyrics*

lit - tle Lord Je - sus laid down His sweet head. The

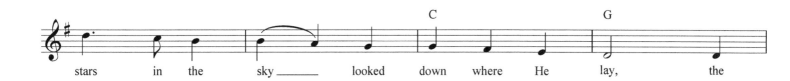

stars in the sky _____ looked down where He lay, the

lit - tle Lord Je - sus, a - sleep on the hay. 2. The there.
3. Be

Additional Lyrics

2. The cattle are lowing, the Baby awakes,
   But little Lord Jesus, no crying He makes.
   I love Thee, Lord Jesus, look down from the sky
   And stay by my cradle 'til morning is nigh.

3. Be near me, Lord Jesus, I ask Thee to stay
   Close by me forever, and love me, I pray.
   Bless all the dear children in Thy tender care,
   And fit us for heaven to live with Thee there.

The Chipmunk Song

Words and Music by Ross Bagdasarian

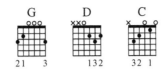

Verse
Happily

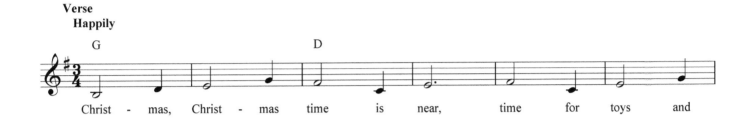

Christ - mas, Christ - mas time is near, time for toys and

time for cheer. We've been good, but we can't last.

Hur - ry, Christ - mas, hur - ry fast! Want a plane that

loops the loop. Me, I want a Hu - la - hoop. We can

hard - ly stand the wait. Please, Christ - mas, don't be late. _____

Christmas Is A-Comin'
(May God Bless You)

Words and Music by Frank Luther

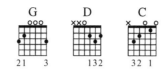

Verse
Moderately

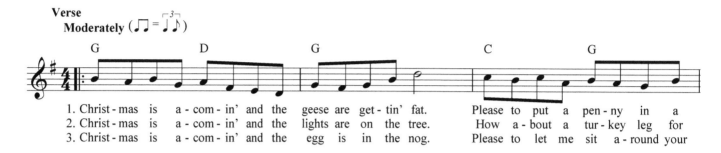

1. Christ-mas is a-com-in' and the geese are get-tin' fat. Please to put a pen-ny in a
2. Christ-mas is a-com-in' and the lights are on the tree. How a-bout a tur-key leg for
3. Christ-mas is a-com-in' and the egg is in the nog. Please to let me sit a-round your

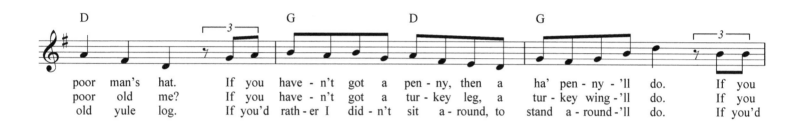

poor man's hat. If you have-n't got a pen-ny, then a ha' pen-ny-'ll do. If you
poor old me? If you have-n't got a tur-key leg, a tur-key wing-'ll do. If you
old yule log. If you'd rath-er I did-n't sit a-round, to stand a-round-'ll do. If you'd

Chorus

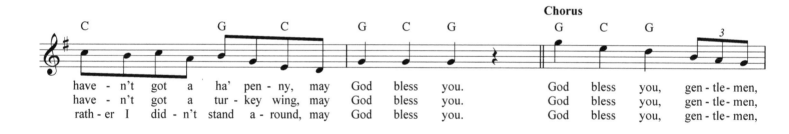

have-n't got a ha' pen-ny, may God bless you. God bless you, gen-tle-men,
have-n't got a tur-key wing, may God bless you. God bless you, gen-tle-men,
rath-er I did-n't stand a-round, may God bless you. God bless you, gen-tle-men,

1., 2.

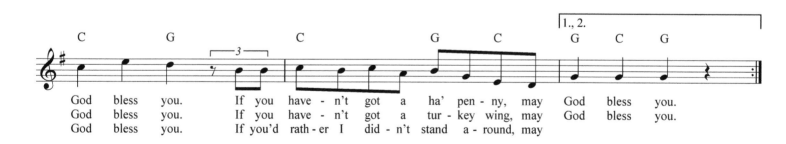

God bless you. If you have-n't got a ha' pen-ny, may God bless you.
God bless you. If you have-n't got a tur-key wing, may God bless you.
God bless you. If you'd rath-er I did-n't stand a-round, may

3.
Outro
Slowly

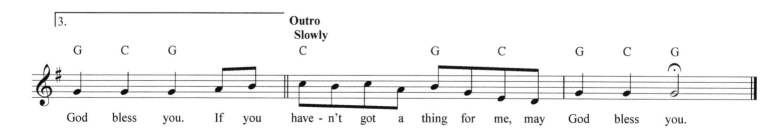

God bless you. If you have-n't got a thing for me, may God bless you.

The First Noel

17th Century English Carol
Music from W. Sandys' *Christmas Carols*

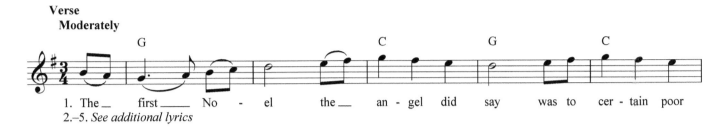

Verse
Moderately

1. The __ first __ No - el the __ an - gel did say was to cer - tain poor
2.–5. *See additional lyrics*

shep - herds in fields as they lay; in __ fields __ where __ they lay __ keep - ing their

sheep, on a cold win - ter's night __ that was __ so deep. No -

Chorus

el, __ No - el, No - el, No - el,

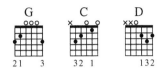

born is the King __ of Is - ra - el.

Additional Lyrics

2. They looked up and saw a star
   Shining in the east, beyond them far.
   And to the earth it gave great light
   And so it continued both day and night.

3. And by the light of that same star,
   Three wise men came from country far;
   To seek for a King was their intent,
   And to follow the star wherever it went.

4. This star drew nigh to the northwest,
   O'er Bethlehem it took its rest;
   And there it did both stop and stay,
   Right over the place where Jesus lay.

5. Then entered in those wise men three,
   Full reverently upon their knee;
   And offered there in His presence,
   Their gold, and myrrh, and frankincense.

The Friendly Beasts

Traditional English Carol

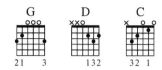

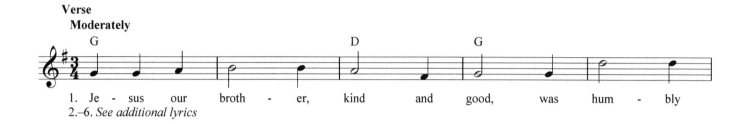

Verse
Moderately

1. Je - sus our broth - er, kind and good, was hum - bly
2.–6. *See additional lyrics*

born in a sta - ble rude; and the friend - ly beasts a - round Him

stood, Je - sus our broth - er, kind and good.

Additional Lyrics

2. "I," said the donkey, shaggy and brown,
   "I carried His mother up hill and down.
   I carried His mother to Bethlehem town."
   "I," said the donkey, shaggy and brown.

3. "I," said the cow, all white and red,
   "I gave him my manger for His bed.
   I gave Him my hay to pillow His head."
   "I," said the cow, all white and red.

4. "I," said the sheep with the curly horn,
   "I gave Him my wool for His blanket warm.
   He wore my coat on Christmas morn."
   "I," said the sheep with the curly horn.

5. "I," said the dove from the rafters high,
   "I cooed Him to sleep that He would not cry.
   We cooed Him to sleep, my mate and I."
   "I," said the dove from the rafters high.

6. Thus every beast by some good spell,
   In the stable dark was glad to tell
   Of the gift he gave Emmanuel,
   The gift he gave Emmanuel.

Go, Tell It on the Mountain

African-American Spiritual
Verses by John W. Work, Jr.

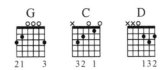

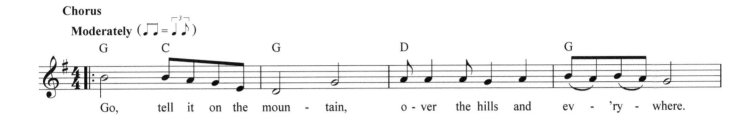

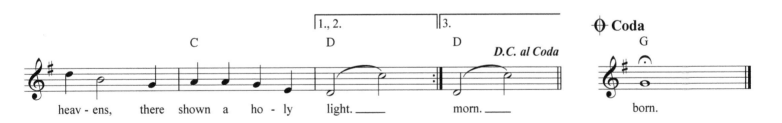

Additional Lyrics

2. The shepherds feared and trembled
When, lo! above the earth
Rang out the angel chorus
That hailed our Savior's birth.

3. Down in a lowly manger
Our humble Christ was born.
And God sent us salvation
That blessed Christmas morn.

Frosty the Snow Man

Words and Music by Steve Nelson and Jack Rollins

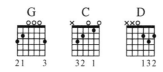

Verse
Moderately fast

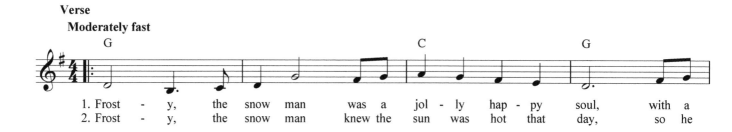

1. Frost - y, the snow man was a jol - ly hap - py soul, with a
2. Frost - y, the snow man knew the sun was hot that day, so he

corn - cob pipe and a but - ton nose and two eyes made out of coal.
said, "Let's run and we'll have some fun now be - fore I melt a - way."

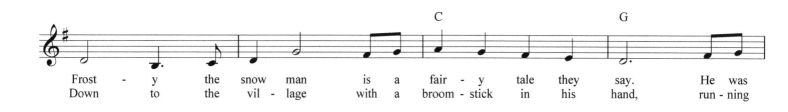

Frost - y the snow man is a fair - y tale they say. He was
Down to the vil - lage with a broom - stick in his hand, run - ning

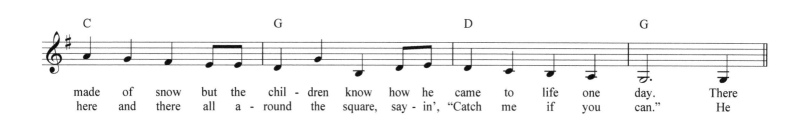

made of snow but the chil - dren know how he came to life one day. There
here and there all a - round the square, say - in', "Catch me if you can." He

Bridge

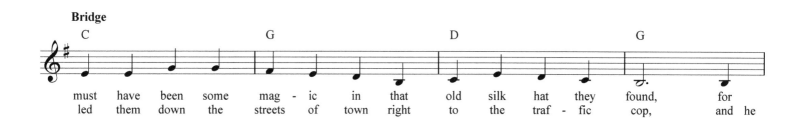

must have been some mag - ic in that old silk hat they found, for
led them down the streets of town right to the traf - fic cop, and he

when they placed it on his head he be-gan to dance a-round. Oh,
on-ly paused a mo-ment when ___ he heard him hol-ler, "Stop!" For

Verse

Frost - y the snow man was a-live as he could be, and the
Frost - y the snow man had to hur-ry on his way, but he

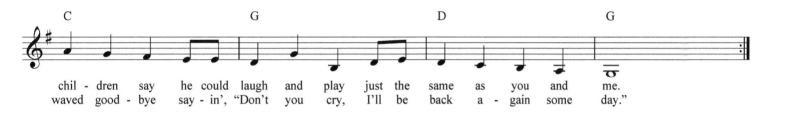

chil - dren say he could laugh and play just the same as you and me.
waved good-bye say-in', "Don't you cry, I'll be back a-gain some day."

Outro

Thump-et - y thump thump, thump-et - y thump thump, look at Frost - y go.

Thump-et - y thump thump, thump-et - y thump thump, o-ver the hills of snow.

Grandma Got Run Over by a Reindeer

Words and Music by Randy Brooks

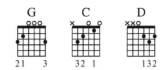

Chorus
Moderately bright

Grand-ma got run o-ver by a rein-deer walk-ing home from our house Christ-mas

Eve. You can say there's no such thing as San-ta, but

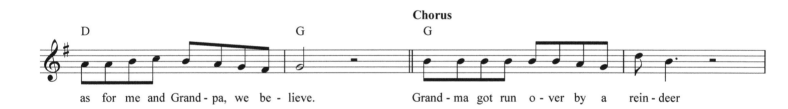

Chorus

as for me and Grand-pa, we be-lieve. Grand-ma got run o-ver by a rein-deer

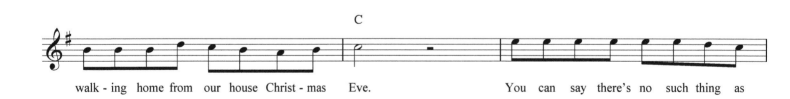

walk-ing home from our house Christ-mas Eve. You can say there's no such thing as

San-ta, but as for me and Grand-pa, we be-lieve.

He Is Born, the Holy Child
(Il est ne, le divin enfant)

Traditional French Carol

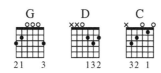

Chorus
Moderately, in 2

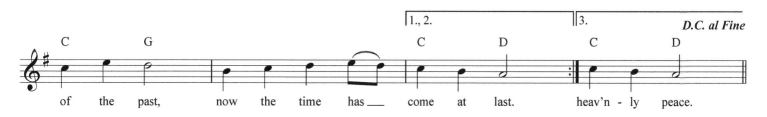

Additional Lyrics

2. Oh, how lovely, oh, how pure,
   Is this perfect Child of heaven.
   Oh, how lovely, oh, how pure,
   Gracious gift of God to man.

3. Jesus, Lord of all the world,
   Coming as a Child among us.
   Jesus, Lord of all the world,
   Grant to us Thy heav'nly peace.

Here Comes Santa Claus
(Right Down Santa Claus Lane)

Words and Music by Gene Autry and Oakley Haldeman

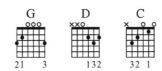

Verse
Moderately, in 2

1. Here comes San - ta Claus! Here comes San - ta Claus! Right down San - ta Claus Lane!
2.–4. *See additional lyrics*

Vix - en and Blitz - en and all his rein - deer are pull - ing on the rein. Bells are ring - ing,

chil - dren sing - ing, all is mer - ry and bright. Hang your stock - ings and

say your prayers, 'cause San - ta Claus comes to - night. night.

Additional Lyrics

2. Here comes Santa Claus! Here comes Santa Claus!
   Right down Santa Claus Lane!
   He's got a bag that is filled with toys
   For the boys and girls again.
   Hear those sleigh bells jingle, jangle,
   What a beautiful sight.
   Jump in bed, cover up your head,
   'Cause Santa Claus comes tonight.

3. Here comes Santa Claus! Here comes Santa Claus!
   Right down Santa Claus Lane!
   He doesn't care if you're rich or poor,
   For he loves you just the same.
   Santa knows that we're God's children;
   That makes ev'rything right.
   Fill your hearts with a Christmas cheer,
   'Cause Santa Claus comes tonight.

4. Here comes Santa Claus! Here comes Santa Claus!
   Right down Santa Claus Lane!
   He'll come around when the chimes ring out;
   Then it's Christmas morn again.
   Peace on earth will come to all
   If we just follow the light.
   Let's give thanks to the Lord above,
   'Cause Santa Claus comes tonight.

The Holly and the Ivy

18th Century English Carol

Verse
Moderately slow

1. The hol - ly and the i - vy, when they are both full grown, of __
2.–5. *See additional lyrics*

all the trees that are in the wood, the __ hol - ly bears the crown. The

Chorus

ris - ing of the sun __ and the run - ning of the deer. The __

play - ing of the mer - ry or - gan, sweet sing - ing of the choir.

Additional Lyrics

2. The holly bears a blossom,
   As white as lily flow'r,
   And Mary bore sweet Jesus Christ,
   To be our sweet Saviour.

3. The holly bears a berry,
   As red as any blood,
   And Mary bore sweet Jesus Christ,
   To do poor sinners good.

4. The holly bears a prickle,
   As sharp as any thorn,
   And Mary bore sweet Jesus Christ,
   On Christmas Day in the morn.

5. The holly bears a bark,
   As bitter as any gall,
   And Mary bore sweet Jesus Christ,
   For to redeem us all.

It Won't Seem Like Christmas
(Without You)

Words and Music by J.A. Balthrop

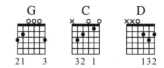

℅ Chorus

Moderately

Oh, it won't seem like Christ - mas, oh, with - out you, for

too man - y miles are be - tween. But if

I get the one thing that I'm wish - ing for,

To Coda ⊕

then I'll see you to - night in my dreams.

Verse

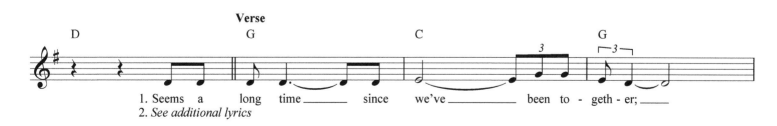

1. Seems a long time since we've been to - geth - er;
2. *See additional lyrics*

it was just a - bout to this time of year.

Looks like it's gon - na be snow - y weath - er.

How I wish that you could be here.

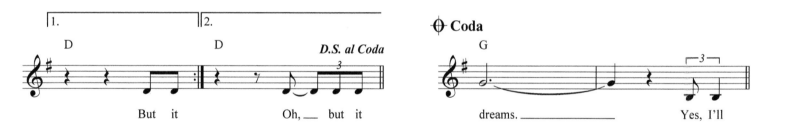

But it   Oh, but it   dreams.   Yes, I'll

Outro   **Slower (♩♩ = ♩♩)**

see you to - night in my dreams.

Additional Lyrics

2. In the distance I hear sleigh bells ringing.
The holly's so pretty this year;
And the carol that somebody's singing
Reminds me of our Christmas last year.

Jingle Bells

Words and Music by J. Pierpont

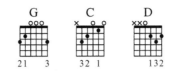

Verse
Brightly, in 2

1. Dash-ing through the snow, in a one-horse o-pen sleigh. O'er the fields we go,
2., 3. *See additional lyrics*

laugh-ing all the way. Bells on bob-tail ring, mak-ing spir-its bright. What fun it is to

Chorus

ride and sing a sleigh-ing song to-night! Oh! Jin-gle bells, jin-gle bells, jin-gle all the

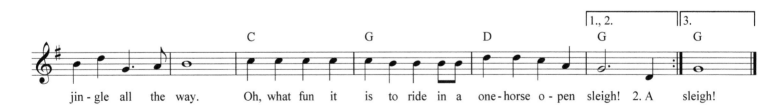

way. Oh, what fun it is to ride in a one-horse o-pen sleigh! __ Jin-gle bells, jin-gle bells,

1., 2. **3.**

jin-gle all the way. Oh, what fun it is to ride in a one-horse o-pen sleigh! 2. A sleigh!

Additional Lyrics

2. A day or two ago, I thought I'd take a ride,
And soon Miss Fannie Bright was sitting by my side.
The horse was lean and lank, misfortune seemed his lot.
He got into a drifted bank and we, we got upsot! Oh!

3. Now the ground is white, go it while you're young.
Take the girls tonight and sing this sleighing song.
Just get a bobtail bay, two-forty for his speed.
Then hitch him to an open sleigh and crack, you'll take the lead! Oh!

Joy to the World

Words by Isaac Watts
Music by George Frideric Handel
Adapted by Lowell Mason

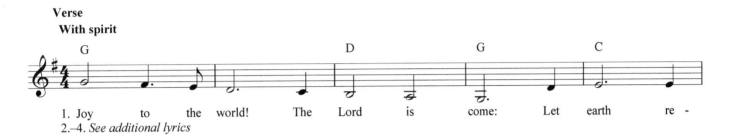

Verse
With spirit

1. Joy to the world! The Lord is come: Let earth re-
2.–4. *See additional lyrics*

ceive her King. Let ev - 'ry ___ heart ___ pre - pare ___ Him ___

room, ___ and heav'n and na - ture ___ sing, and ___ heav'n and na - ture ___

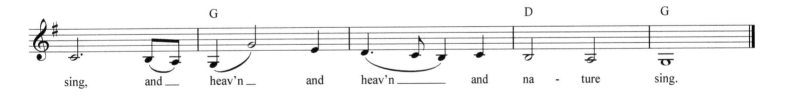

sing, and ___ heav'n ___ and heav'n ___ and na - ture sing.

Additional Lyrics

2. Joy to the earth! The Savior reigns;
   Let men their songs employ
   While fields and floods, rocks, hills and plains
   Repeat the sounding joy,
   Repeat the sounding joy,
   Repeat, repeat the sounding joy.

3. No more let sin and sorrow grow,
   Nor thorns infest the ground.
   He comes to make His blessings flow
   Far as the curse is found,
   Far as the curse is found,
   Far as, far as the curse is found.

4. He rules the world with truth and grace
   And makes the nations prove
   The glories of His righteousness,
   And wonders of His love,
   And wonders of His love,
   And wonders, wonders of His love.

The Little Drummer Boy

Words and Music by Harry Simeone, Henry Onorati and Katherine Davis

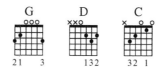

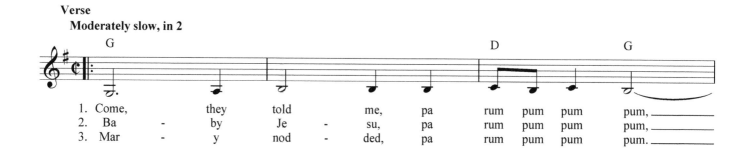

Verse

Moderately slow, in 2

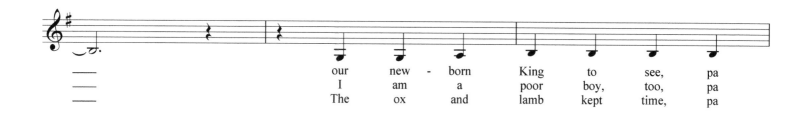

1. Come, they told me, pa rum pum pum pum, _____
2. Ba - by Je - su, pa rum pum pum pum, _____
3. Mar - y nod - ded, pa rum pum pum pum. _____

— our new - born King to see, pa
— I am a poor boy, too, pa
The ox and lamb kept time, pa

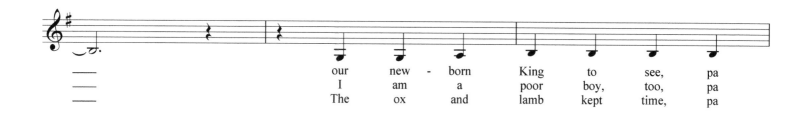

rum pum pum pum. _____ Our fin - est
rum pum pum pum. _____ I have no
rum pum pum pum. _____ I played my

gifts we bring, pa rum pum pum pum, _____
gift to bring, pa rum pum pum pum, _____
drum for Him, pa rum pum pum pum. _____

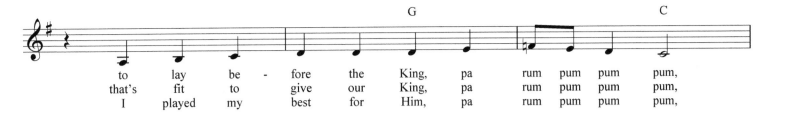

to   lay   be -   fore   the   King,   pa   rum   pum   pum   pum,

that's   fit   to   give   our   King,   pa   rum   pum   pum   pum,

I   played   my   best   for   Him,   pa   rum   pum   pum   pum,

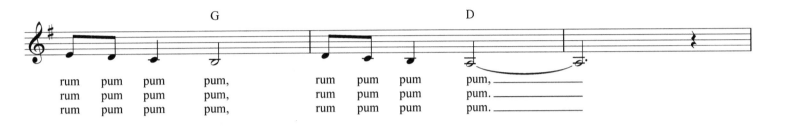

rum   pum   pum   pum,   rum   pum   pum   pum.

rum   pum   pum   pum,   rum   pum   pum   pum.

rum   pum   pum   pum,   rum   pum   pum   pum.

so   to   hon -   or   Him,   pa   rum   pum   pum   pum,

Shall   I   play   for   you,   pa   rum   pum   pum   pum,

Then   He   smiled   at   me,   pa   rum   pum   pum   pum,

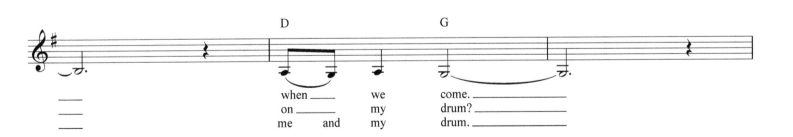

when   we   come.

on   my   drum?

me   and   my   drum.

Mary's Little Boy

Words and Music by Massie Patterson and Sammy Heyward

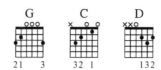

Verse
Moderately bright

1. Mar - y she had a lit - tle boy, __ Mar - y she had a lit - tle boy, __
2., 3. *See additional lyrics*

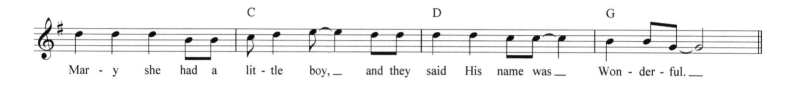

Mar - y she had a lit - tle boy, __ and they said His name was __ Won - der - ful. __

Pre-Chorus

He came down from heav - en, He came down from heav - en,

He came down from heav - en, and they said His name was Won - der - ful. __

Chorus

Oh, yes, Won - der - ful. __ Oh, yes, Coun - sel - or. __

Won - der - ful, __ Coun - sel - or, __ He came down __ from heav - en.

Additional Lyrics

2. Soldiers looked for the little boy,
   Soldiers looked for the little boy,
   Soldiers looked for the little boy,
   And they said His name was Wonderful.

3. Wise men came running from the East,
   Wise men came running from the East,
   Wise men came running from the East,
   And they said His name was Wonderful.

A Merry, Merry Christmas to You

Music and Lyrics by Johnny Marks

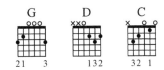

Chorus
Spirited, in 1

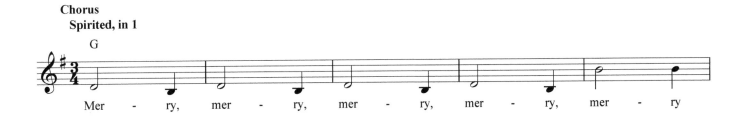

Mer - ry, mer - ry, mer - ry, mer - ry, mer - ry

Christ - mas to you. _____ May each day be ver - y,

ver - y hap - py all the year through. _____ A -

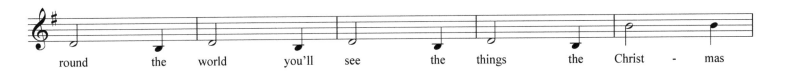

round the world you'll see the things the Christ - mas

spir - it can do. _____ Bells will be ring - ing with

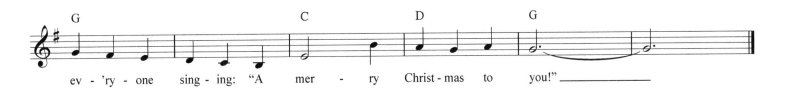

ev - 'ry - one sing - ing: "A mer - ry Christ - mas to you!" _____

Merry Christmas, Baby

Words and Music by Lou Baxter and Johnny Moore

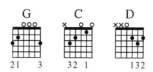

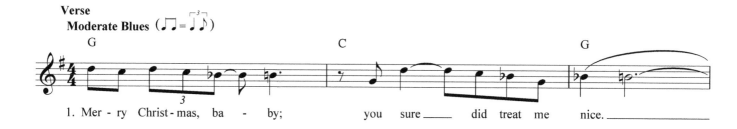

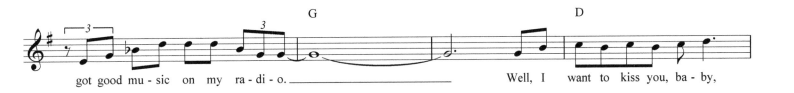

got good mu - sic on my ra - di - o. _____ Well, I want to kiss you, ba - by,

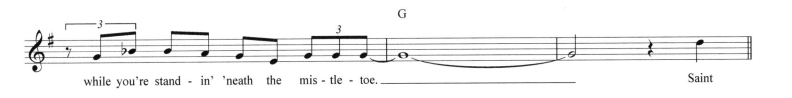

while you're stand - in' 'neath the mis - tle - toe. _____ Saint

Outro-Verse

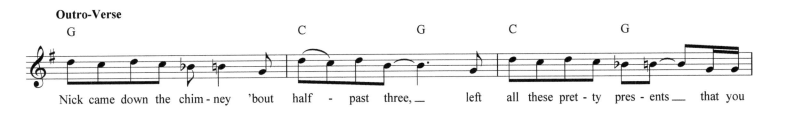

Nick came down the chim - ney 'bout half - past three, __ left all these pret - ty pres - ents __ that you

see be - fore me. __ Mer - ry Christ - mas, lit - tle ba - by; you sure __ been good to

me. _____ I have - n't had a drink this morn - in', __ but I'm

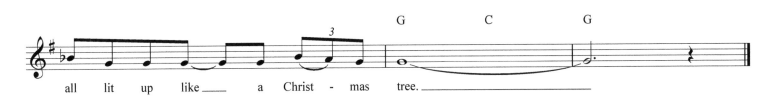

all lit up like __ a Christ - mas tree. _____

O Christmas Tree

Traditional German Carol

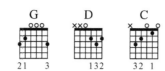

Additional Lyrics

2. O Christmas tree, O Christmas tree,
   Much pleasure doth thou bring me!
   O Christmas tree, O Christmas tree,
   Much pleasure doth thou bring me!
   For every year the Christmas tree
   Brings to us all both joy and glee.
   O Christmas tree, O Christmas tree,
   Much pleasure doth thou bring me!

3. O Christmas tree, O Christmas tree,
   Thy candles shine out brightly!
   O Christmas tree, O Christmas tree,
   Thy candles shine out brightly!
   Each bough doth hold its tiny light
   That makes each toy to sparkle bright.
   O Christmas tree, O Christmas tree,
   Thy candles shine out brightly.

Once in Royal David's City

Words by Cecil F. Alexander
Music by Henry J. Gauntlett

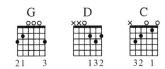

Verse
Moderately

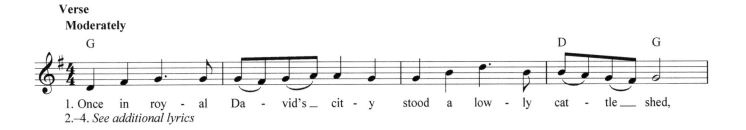

1. Once in roy - al Da - vid's city stood a low - ly cat - tle __ shed,
2.–4. *See additional lyrics*

where a moth - er laid __ her __ ba - by in a man - ger for __ His __ bed.

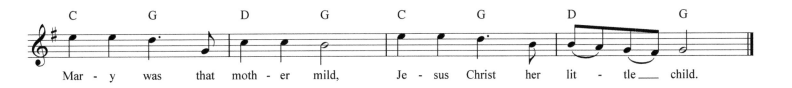

Mar - y was that moth - er mild, Je - sus Christ her lit - tle __ child.

Additional Lyrics

2. He came down to earth from heaven,
   Who is God and Lord of all,
   And His shelter was a stable,
   And His cradle was a stall:
   With the poor, and mean, and lowly,
   Lived on earth our Savior holy.

3. Jesus is our childhood's pattern,
   Day by day like us He grew;
   He was little, weak and helpless,
   Tears and smiles like us He knew:
   And He feeleth for our sadness,
   And He shareth in our gladness.

4. And our eyes at last shall see Him,
   Through his own redeeming love.
   For the child so dear and gentle
   Is our Lord in heav'n above.
   And He leads His children on
   To the place where He is gone.

Shake Me I Rattle
(Squeeze Me I Cry)

Words and Music by Hal Hackady and Charles Naylor

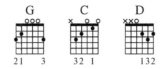

Verse

Moderately slow

1. I was pass - ing by a toy shop on the
(2.) called an - oth - er toy shop on a
(3.) late and snow was fall - ing as the

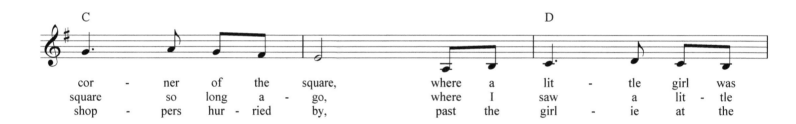

cor - ner of the square, where a lit - tle girl was
square so long a - go, where I saw a lit - tle
shop - pers hur - ried by, past the girl - ie at the

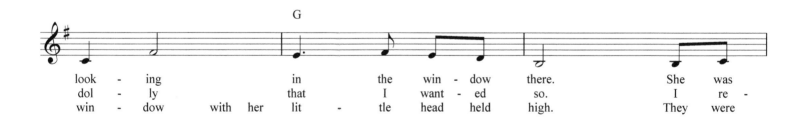

look - ing in the win - dow there. She was
dol - ly that I want - ed so. I re -
win - dow with her lit - tle head held high. They were

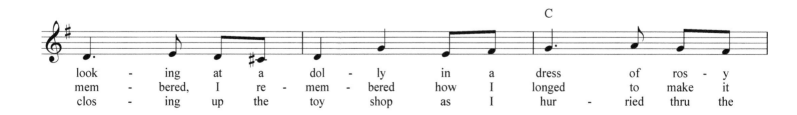

look - ing at a dol - ly in a dress of ros - y
mem - bered, I re - mem - bered how I longed to make it
clos - ing up the toy shop as I hur - ried thru the

red,   and a - round   the   pret - ty   dol - ly   hung   a
mine,   and a - round   that   oth - er   dol - ly   hung   an -
door,   just in   time   to   buy   the   dol - ly   that   her

Chorus

lit - tle   sign   that   said: Shake   me,   I
oth - er   lit - tle   sign: Shake   me,   I
heart was long - ing   for.   Shake   me,   I

rat - tle.   Squeeze   me,   I   cry.   As   I
rat - tle.   Squeeze   me,   I   cry.   I   had
rat - tle.   Squeeze   me,   I   cry.   And   I

stood there be - side   her,   I   could hear   her
count - ed my   pen - nies,   that we both   had   just   a   pen - ny
gave her the   dol - ly   that we both   had longed to

sigh.   }
shy.   }   Shake   me,   I   rat - tle.
buy.   }

Squeeze me, I   cry.   Please take   me   home   and

1., 2.   3.

love ____ me. ____   2. I   re - ____
                  3. It was

Silent Night

Words by Joseph Mohr
Translated by John F. Young
Music by Franz X. Gruber

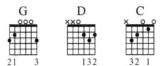

Verse
Slowly

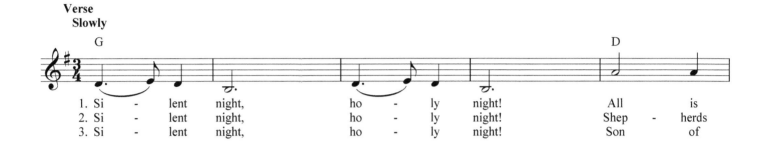

1. Si - lent night, ho - ly night! All is
2. Si - lent night, ho - ly night! Shep - herds
3. Si - lent night, ho - ly night! Son of

calm, all is bright 'round yon Vir - gin
quake at the sight. Glo - ries stream ____ from
God, love's pure light. Ra - diant beams ____ from

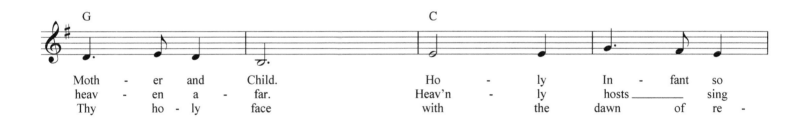

Moth - er and Child. Ho - ly In - fant so
heav - en a - far. Heav'n - ly hosts ____ sing
Thy ho - ly face with the dawn of re -

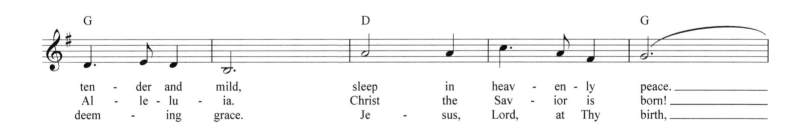

ten - der and mild, sleep in heav - en - ly peace. ____
Al - le - lu - ia. Christ the Sav - ior is born! ____
deem - ing grace. Je - sus, Lord, at Thy birth, ____

____ Sleep ____ in heav - en - ly peace. ____
____ Christ ____ the Sav - ior is born! ____
____ Je - sus, Lord, at Thy birth. ____

Silver Bells

from the Paramount Picture THE LEMON DROP KID
Words and Music by Jay Livingston and Ray Evans

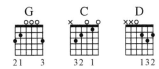

Moderately **Verse**

1. Cit - y side - walks, bus - y side - walks dressed in hol - i - day style, in the
(2.) street - lights, e - ven stop - lights blink a bright red and green, as the

air there's a feel - ing of Christ - mas.   Chil - dren laugh - ing, peo - ple
shop - pers rush home with their treas - ures.   Hear the snow crunch, see the

pass - ing, meet - ing smile af - ter smile, and on ev - 'ry street cor - ner you'll
kids bunch, this is San - ta's big scene, and a - bove all this bus - tle you'll

Chorus

hear: _____⎱ Sil - ver bells, _____ sil - ver bells. _____
hear: _____⎰

___ It's Christ - mas time in the cit - y.

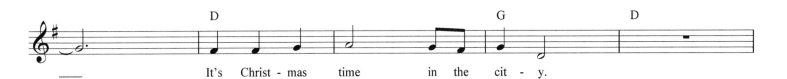

Ring - a - ling, _____ hear them ring. _____ Soon it will

1.   2.

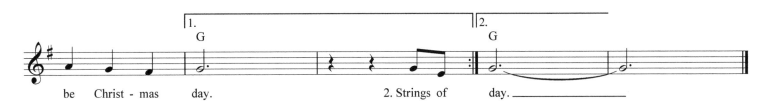

be Christ - mas day.   2. Strings of   day. _____

What a Merry Christmas This Could Be

Words and Music by Hank Cochran and Harlan Howard

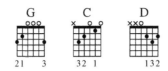

What a mer - ry Christ - mas this could be if you __

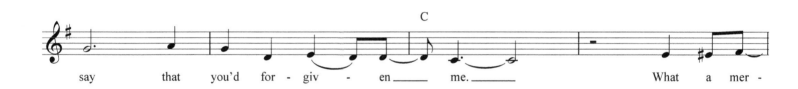

__ would just come back __ to __ me __ and

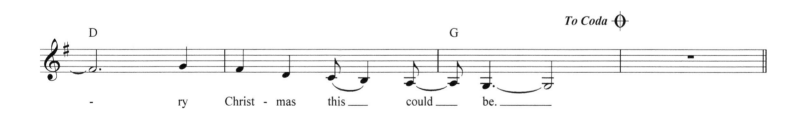

say that you'd for - giv - en __ me. __ What a mer -

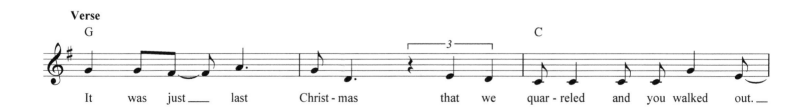

- ry Christ - mas this __ could __ be. __

It was just __ last Christ - mas that we quar - reled and you walked out. __

I knew ____ I was wrong, ____ but you'd ____ come

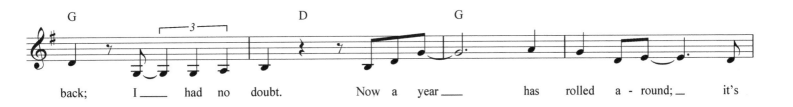

back; I ____ had no doubt. Now a year ____ has rolled a - round; ____ it's

Christ - mas once a - gain, and what I'd give if

D.S. al Coda   ⊕ **Coda**

you'd _ come _ walk - in' ____ in. What a mer -   What a mer -

Outro

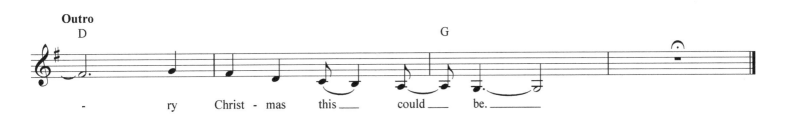

- ry Christ - mas this ____ could ____ be. ____

While Shepherds Watched Their Flocks

Words by Nahum Tate
Music by George Frideric Handel

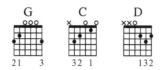

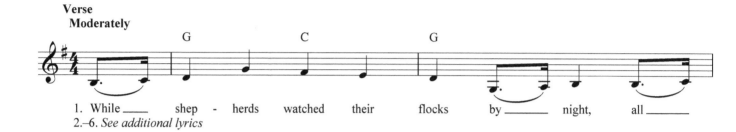

Additional Lyrics

2. "Fear not!" said he, for mighty dread
   Had seized their troubled mind.
   "Glad tidings of great joy I bring
   To you and all mankind,
   To you and all mankind.

3. "To you, in David's town this day,
   Is born of David's line,
   The Savior, who is Christ the Lord;
   And this shall be the sign,
   And this shall be the sign:

4. "The heav'nly Babe you there shall find
   To human view displayed,
   All meanly wrapped in swathing bands
   And in a manger laid,
   And in a manger laid."

5. Thus spake the seraph, and forthwith
   Appeared a shining throng
   Of angels praising God on high,
   Who thus addressed their song,
   Who thus addressed their song:

6. "All glory be to God on high,
   And to the earth be peace.
   Good will henceforth from heav'n to men,
   Begin and never cease,
   Begin and never cease!"